Pursuing the
Mind of Christ

It is a journey

WRITTEN BY

DALE WARD

Pursuing the Mind of Christ

Published by Freedom Quest Publishing

Copyright © 2011 by Freedom Quest Ministries

ISBN 978-0-9848215-0-1

Printed in the United States of America

Order books at: www.freedomquest.org

I dedicate this book to my family, especially to my
children and their spouses, Scott and Shelley Ward,
Phillip and Jennifer Powell; and my grandchildren
Ryan, Jason, Amanda, Joel, and Katie.

Contents

Acknowledgements

Reverends Alan Scott and Dr. Gary L. Durham, who I served with in the pastorate, and are dear friends, taught me many of these biblical principles.

Don Fischer, who owns Fischer Creative, and is a very close Christian brother and friend, designed the interior illustrations and the book's cover.

Lee Synnott, who is a very close Christian brother, and friend, encouraged me in many ways, and he guided me through all the publishing steps.

Maury Regan who took his time and resources to take a lot of pictures that allowed us to select one for the back cover.

Barbara Ward, who is my dear wife, has faithfully traveled full time with me all over the country while I regularly preached these biblical principles, and she lived full time in a motorhome while I traveled. She has supported me for over forty years including being my only caretaker after my stroke.

Introduction

My daughter was reminiscing the other day about one particular vacation that we took several years ago. Although she was very young then, she remembers that when she inquired about our arrival time, I said that we had only about fifteen minutes remaining. She then inquired again in about fifteen minutes, and I said that we had about two hours. Without a doubt, she was very confused. You see, I was also very confused. The first time she asked, I thought we were farther along than we were. In the meantime, I saw one of those green information signs that revealed the number of miles to our destination.

A similar confusion can exist with us and our spiritual journey. We can think that we are somewhere we are not. We need a green information sign. We need a copy of the Word of God as a map to tell us exactly where we are on our journey. The Bible tells us that the journey or the road is not for everybody. In Isaiah 35:8 we are told "and a highway will be there; it will be called the Way of Holiness. The unclean will not journey on it, it will be for those who walk on that Way, wicked fools will not go about on it" In the New Testament, specifically John 3:20,

Jesus says something similar "Everyone who does evil hates the light, and will not come into the light for fear that their deeds will be exposed." You see, we need the light to be our information sign to tell us exactly where we are on our spiritual journey. Not everyone will be interested in coming into the light to see where they are. But, knowing where we are is not good enough. As embarrassing and frustrating as it may have been to realize that I actually did not know where I was on my road trip, being open to the revelation that the information sign brought to me was rather freeing. In fact, we need to be open to the revelation that God's Word can bring to us.

It does not matter how long we have been on the journey, we all need to be open for experiencing more truth and the freedom that comes with it. When you are finished with this book, I don't want you to have gained intellectual knowledge only; I want you to have gained freedom. We are told in John what it really means to be a follower of Jesus Christ, and how we can have freedom. The Bible tells us in John 8:31-32, "If you hold to my teaching, you are really my disciples. Then you will know the truth, and the truth will set you free." We need to take the time to unpack these verses, because a proper understanding is crucial for us to experience the spiritual growth that this book has to offer.

First of all, these verses tell us that freedom is only possible for those individuals who are devoted to the teaching of Jesus. The verse tells us that we are really a disciple if we hold to Jesus' teaching. A *disciple* is a learner or a pupil. *Hold* means to continue, to abide, to remain, to endure, or to last. So to be really a disciple, we must continue or last as a learner of the teaching of Jesus. *Teaching* means the sayings of God. It should be noted that the word is in the singular. We should realize that Jesus does not have multiple teachings that we can choose; he has one teaching that we need to continuously be devoted to what we have learned in order to be considered a disciple. The word *then* is a time-sequence word that simply means a time order of events exists. As long as we continue as a learner of the teaching of Jesus, then we will know the truth, and the truth will set us free. The word *know* actually means an experiential knowledge. In other words, I might have the formal education in some discipline, but I don't really have "knowledge" until I have a few years of experience working on the job. For example, my trainer, Dustin, has completed all the formal education to become an exercise physiologist, but he didn't really "know" exercise training until he began training people. In fact, an intern who is almost finished with his formal education works alongside Dustin in an internship program. It is fair to say that the interns might have as much, or even more, formal education as Dustin, but they don't have the *knowledge* that Dustin has. Obviously, all of them will probably gain more knowledge every day they spend being faithful to the teaching they received in their formal education. This is the way it works in our spiritual life. After we decide to continue to be a learner of the teaching of Jesus, then we will experience the truth, and the truth we experience or obey will set us free.

I want you to read this book with a goal of experiencing the truth. As I said earlier, I don't want you to gain intellectual knowledge only; I want you to gain freedom. This will also develop a mind of Christ.

Chapter One

The Beginning

At one time, Barbara, my wife, and I were conducting services in the northern part of the United States in the winter months. I would sometimes take a rest in the afternoon in order to be ready to minister in the church service that night. Occasionally, with my eyes closed, I would begin to visually dream that I was in warm weather with palm trees and beaches. But when I opened my eyes and looked outside, I would see that it had started snowing. I realized that not only was I not in the place I had dreamed; I had not even started my journey! A character in the Bible had a similar experience. His name is Nicodemus, and his story can be found in John 3.

> Now there was a Pharisee, a man named Nicodemus who was a member of the Jewish ruling council. He came to Jesus at night and said, "Rabbi, we know that you are a teacher who has come from God. For no one could perform the signs you are doing if God were not with him."

Jesus replied, "Very truly I tell you, no one can see the kingdom of God unless they are born again."

"How can someone be born when they are old?" Nicodemus asked. "Surely they cannot enter a second time into their mother's womb to be born!"

Jesus answered, "Very truly I tell you, no one can enter the kingdom of God unless they are born of water and the Spirit. Flesh gives birth to flesh, but the Spirit gives birth to spirit. You should not be surprised at my saying, 'You must be born again.' The wind blows wherever it pleases. You hear its sound, but you cannot tell where it comes from or where it is going. So it is with everyone born of the Spirit."

"How can this be?" Nicodemus asked.

"You are Israel's teacher," said Jesus, "and do you not understand these things? Very truly I tell you, we speak of what we know, and we testify to what we have seen, but still you people do not accept our testimony. I have spoken to you of earthly things and you do not believe; how then will you believe if I speak of heavenly things? No one has ever gone into heaven except the one who came from heaven—the Son of Man. Just as Moses lifted up the snake in the wilderness, so the Son of Man must be lifted up, that everyone who believes may have eternal life in him."

For God so loved the world that he gave his one and only Son, that whoever believes in him shall not perish but have eternal life. For God did not send his Son into the world to condemn the world, but to save the world through him. Whoever believes in him is not condemned, but whoever does not believe stands condemned already because they have not believed in the name of God's one and only Son. (John 3:1-19)

For us to get the most out of this passage of scripture we really need a better understanding of Nicodemus.

From this passage we know he was a Pharisee. This means he was a member of a sect of people that thought they had the correct understanding on how to get into heaven. He was a very religious person and probably was a very kind and generous man. In fact, he was probably in the church building every time there was a service. We are also told that he was a member of the Jewish ruling council. This means he was a leader, or commander or chief, of the Jewish people. He was probably very rich financially, and very powerful in his community. He was also probably well educated. The Bible tells us that he was Israel's teacher. He was a teacher of the Jewish people. He probably taught others the requirements to get into heaven.

Although there are a number of possible reasons he might have come to Jesus at night, we don't actually know why, because the story doesn't tell us. What we do know is that Nicodemus told Jesus that they knew he had to be God's teacher because of the special things he was doing.

Although Nicodemus doesn't ask Jesus a question, Jesus just cuts to the chase. He starts his conversation by saying "very truly," In other translations it might be translated "truly, truly," but regardless of the translation, when Jesus says this it means that you should highlight what he is about to say, or you should underline it, or you should put it in bold letters. Jesus is saying that you should pay close attention to what he is about to say because it is very important. Then Jesus tells Nicodemus that no one can enter into heaven unless they are born again. Well, this is quite different from what Nicodemus thought or taught as was one of the requirements. Then Nicodemus asked the question "How can someone be born when they are old? . . . Surely they cannot enter a second time into their mother's womb to be born!" Some people think Nicodemus was being a smart aleck, but I personally think that he was asking Jesus a very legitimate question. We should ask the same question. He was very confused, because what Jesus was saying was very different from what Nicodemus was taught and believed, and Nicodemus was thinking about the physical realm and a physical birth. Nicodemus would have believed that whether or not he would make it into heaven really depended on his personal actions.

If we want to know how to be born again, it might help to investigate how we were born the first time. And for us to do that, we need to look at how all of mankind was born the first time. We need to go to the book of the beginnings, which is the very first book of the Bible, the book of Genesis. We are told in the first part of Genesis 2:7, "Then the LORD God formed a man from the dust of the ground and breathed into his nostrils the breath of life…" So, we can learn from this scripture that mankind is essentially made of two components—a

physical part and a spiritual part. Of course, the physical part is the visible part that we can see, such as our skin, muscles, bones, and so on. The spiritual part is the invisible part that we cannot see such as our will, cognition, and conscious. In the field of theology this is known as the *dichotomy* of man. There are two essential parts. This is very important to remember, because it might make a difference in the way we deal with our problems. If we cannot prove that our problem originates as a physical problem, then it must be a spiritual problem. However, when the two parts are brought together, a synergy or something special happens. The remainder of the verse tells us, "and the man became a living being." The "living being," which is the soul of man, was created when the spiritual part and the physical part came together. So mankind

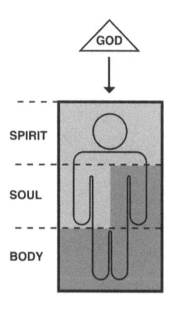

functions with three parts, which is known theologically as the *trichotomy* of man—spirit, soul, and body. The soul of mankind is the personality or identity of the person, and it is made of part visible, or body, and part invisible, or spirit. There is a temptation to spend more resources changing the physical part than the spiritual part when we want to change our identity.

The Bible tells us that God created mankind in his image and his likeness. In the first part of Genesis 1:26, it states this: "Then God said, 'Let us make man in our image, in our likeness, and let them rule over the fish of the sea and the birds of the air, over the livestock, over all the earth, and over all the creatures that move along the ground.'" What does this verse mean? The Hebrew word translated as "image" is *tselem*, and it means "shape, resemblance, figure, shadow." We resem-

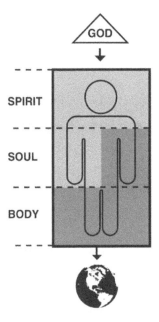

ble the Godhead in our nature, so we were created to have certain capacities. Being born in the image of God makes you very special, and it really doesn't matter what others might say. The Hebrew word translated as "likeness" is *demooth*, which means, "model, shape, fashion, similitude, and bodily resemblance." God originally created mankind so that the capacities would function similar to or like God's capacities.

God put his image and likeness in the soul of man. God has the capacity to make choices that is the "will." So God gave to man the same capacity: will. God has the capacity to think that is "reason." So God gave to man the same capacity: reason. God has the capacity to feel that is "emotion." So God gave to man the same capacity: emotion.

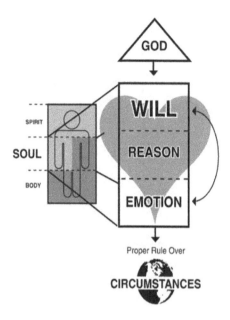

God went a step further. He put his likeness in the soul of man. This would allow man to use the capacities like God does. Mankind would make choices like God, mankind would think like God, and mankind would have feelings like God. When the capacities function as they were created like God's then three things can happen. The capacities will be oriented in the proper order—will, reason, then emotions. We will have a mind of Christ, and God as a Spirit can give us instructions so we can properly have dominion over the circumstances of life.

But something happened. The story in Genesis tells us that after God created the first man, Adam, he placed him in the Garden of Eden, where God created Eve and where all of Adam's and Eve's needs would be met. "And the LORD God commanded the man, 'You are free to eat from any tree in the

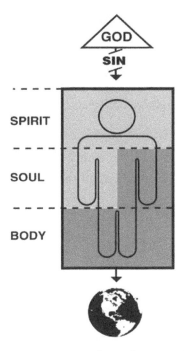

garden; but you must not eat from the tree of the knowledge of good and evil, for when you eat of it you will surely die.'" (Genesis 2:16-17)

Satan, in the form of a snake, came to Eve and appealed to her capacity of reason. Eve thought about what Satan had to say for a moment too long. He got her to question what God had actually said about the forbidden fruit, along with the consequences of eating the fruit. Well, after a little rationalization, Eve ate some of the forbidden fruit and then gave some to Adam to eat. Do you know what happened then? Just as God said, they died. You might say, "But they didn't die because I continue to read about them in the Bible." Well, we need to use the biblical definition of death, and the biblical definition is the separation from the source of life. God is the source of life. He is the source of everything we need. Because of their disobedience, which is considered sin, God expelled Adam and Eve from the Garden of Eden–from his presence, his provision, and his protection. Sin will always separate us from God.

This separation turned mankind upside down. No longer did God rule their lives. The circumstances of life ruled or controlled Adam and Eve. In fact, all the capacities were upside

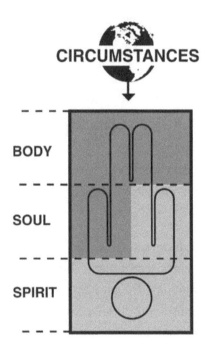

down too. When Adam and Eve disobeyed, sin came into the world, which we refer to as the *fall of man*, and the likeness of God was lost. The image, those capacities that enabled man to make choices, think, and have feelings, were maintained. Adam

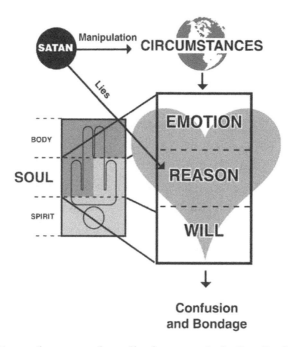

and Eve no longer made godly choices only, had godly thoughts only, or had godly feelings only, but they still had the capacities of will, reason, and emotion. The image was not lost in the fall of man, but the likeness was. Our goal over time should be to have the likeness, which is the mind of Christ, restored. This is the journey that requires a starting point.

The story in Genesis continues. It tells us that because of the committed sin, Adam's and Eve's eyes were opened and they realized that they were naked. They were ashamed, so they made fig leaves to cover themselves. Because they were afraid of God, due to their nakedness, they ran. We also have a tendency to feel shameful when we are guilty of disobedience. We also might become fearful of God and run from him. The

Bible tells us that God called for Adam and asked where he was, and God asked Adam why he was hiding. Now, do you think that God needed to ask Adam these questions for his own knowledge? Absolutely not! God might have wanted Adam to come to the realization of where he was and the reason he was there. Adam needed a green information sign! God also asked Adam how he knew he was naked. In other words, God was asking Adam where his source of reality and his identity was coming from. God knew that the information had not come from him. You see, it couldn't have, because Adam's and Eve's sin separated them from God and him being their source of knowledge. Since they were separated from the true source of knowledge, they had to rely on the physical realm and their physical senses—what they could see, hear, feel, taste, and smell—for their reality. Adam and Eve had become emotionally driven and circumstantially controlled. Their lives were turned upside down, and their likeness of God was lost. In this condition, Satan can communicate lies to the capacity of reason, which will create certain emotions, and then he can manipulate the circumstances to validate the lies. This allows Satan to get mankind to make certain choices with their wills that can lead to confusion and bondage. These emotionally driven or circumstantially controlled choices can lead to more lies, manipulation, and confusion, and then the cycle repeats itself. The Bible tells us that all of mankind was born separated from God because of Adam's and Eve's sin, "even though every inclination of his heart is evil from childhood" (Genesis 8:21). You might say that we were all born spiritually upside down and the likeness of God is missing. This is why the passage tells us "Flesh gives birth to flesh, but the Spirit gives birth to spirit." (John 3:5-7). Yes, we have been born physically, but we must be born again spiritually if we want to get into heaven. We must be born again!

Jesus then refers to a story about Moses that is found in Numbers.

> They traveled from Mount Hor along the route to the Red Sea, to go around Edom. But the people grew impatient on the way; they spoke against God and against Moses, and said, "Why have you brought us up out of Egypt to die in the desert? There is no bread! There is no water! And we detest this miserable food!"
>
> Then the LORD sent venomous snakes among them; they bit the people and many Israelites died. The people came to Moses and said, "We sinned when we spoke against the LORD and against you. Pray that the LORD will take the snakes away from us." So Moses prayed for the people.
>
> The LORD said to Moses, "Make a snake and put it up on a pole; anyone who is bitten can look at it and live." So Moses made a bronze snake and put it up on a pole. Then when anyone was bitten by a snake and looked at the bronze snake, he lived. (Numbers 21:4-9)

Although I think this passage explains what Jesus means, allow me to give a contemporary explanation. Because of his great mercy, God made a way for the sinning people to be saved. Some of the people in belief looked at the snake replica that Moses raised on the pole, and they did not die of the snake bites. Although we are not told, I am sure that some people refused to believe and look at the raised snake replica. They probably thought it was a pretty uneducated approach to deal with a snake bite. Do you know what happened to those individuals? They died.

Jesus then tells us that he must be lifted up on a cross similar to the way Moses lifted the snake replica. "Just as Moses lifted up the snake in the wilderness, so the Son of Man must be lift-

ed up, that everyone who believes may have eternal life in him" (John 3:14). You might say that all of us were born with a snake bite and are experiencing death until we turn in belief to Jesus, who was raised on a cross. We can have eternal life, be born again, and go to heaven with this simple belief.

We are told that God loves everybody in the world and gave his son as a gift to die on a cross so that mankind would have a way to be reconnected to the source of life and not die of our snake bite. "For God so loved the world that he gave his one and only Son, that whoever believes in him shall not perish but have eternal life." (John 3:16)

We are also told that Jesus was not sent to earth to condemn or judge us, but he came to save us. We condemn ourselves if we refuse to believe, "For God did not send his Son into the world to condemn the world, but to save the world through him. Whoever believes in him is not condemned, but whoever does not believe stands condemned already because they have not believed in the name of God's one and only Son" (John 3:17-18).

The meaning of *believe* in this context might be different from what we think. It is not intellectual knowledge only; it is also experiential knowledge (*ginosko*). It reminds me of the tightrope walker at Niagara Falls on a very windy and foggy day. Although there are strong gusts of wind and a lot of mist due to the fog and the water falls, the walker proceeds all the way across the falls and back on the tight cable while pushing a wheelbarrow. When he has returned to the starting point, he finds that a crowd of people has gathered. They all give their approval by clapping loudly. He asks them if they think he can push a person in the wheelbarrow on the same journey in the same perilous conditions. They all give their approval by clapping and shouting loudly. In response the man scans the crowd and says, "Someone should get in." You see, we might intellectually believe that Jesus was born of the virgin Mary, died on a cross for our sins, and was raised from the dead three days later, but we don't really believe until we are willing to get in the wheelbarrow.

At least three characteristics exist in a person's life who has been born again.

1. The individual will have a testimony. This new birth was not forced on them, but it required them to make a choice with their wills when God invited them in to a relation-

ship with Jesus. This did not happen in their sleep, and they should know approximately when and where it happened. They should have a testimony. When I ask people to tell me about when they became a Christian, and all they tell me is how their parents took them to church every Sunday since they came home from the hospital as babies, well, I get a little concerned and probe a little more, because I don't want them to be like Nicodemus. They must be born again and have a testimony of the event.

2. The individual will have a love for the truth and the light. "But whoever lives by the truth comes into the light" (John 3:21a). They will long for a green information sign. No longer will they love the darkness, but they will want to travel on the "highway of holiness." They will have a strong desire to do what is right.

3. They will have a desire for Jesus to be their King. We are birthed into a kingdom when we are born again. A kingdom is hard for those of us in the United States to relate to because of the type of government we live under. A kingdom has a king, and he decides the rules of the kingdom. In a kingdom, there are no referendums or elections to change the leaders or the rules. There will be a desire for Jesus to rule.

You still might wonder if you have been born again. I suggest that you pause and ask Jesus, "Have I been born again?"

After that, you might wonder how you hear God. Well, although there are a lot of different ways, I suggest that in this situation you should imagine a kite string is tied around your chest with the kite flying on a windy day. If you feel a tug on your chest, as if there were gusts of wind tightening the kite string, this may be God inviting you to be born again.

If you decide that you should pray a prayer to be born again, here is one you can use. I do suggest that you pray your prayer out loud.

PRAYER to be BORN AGAIN

Dear Heavenly Father,

Thank you for inviting me to be born again. I agree that I am a sinner and am separated from you as the source of life because of my sin. I need to be born again. I believe that because of your love for me, you have given your son, Jesus Christ, as a gift to die on a cross for my sins. I want Jesus' forgiveness of my sins, and I will turn from my way of life to walk in the light and down the highway of holiness. I want Jesus to lead me as my King.

In Jesus' name I pray,

AMEN

If you prayed this prayer to become born again, I encourage you to tell someone who has already started the journey so they can help you on your walk.

CHAPTER 1 and INTRODUCTION
STUDY QUESTIONS

Introduction

1. What should we use to determine where we are on our spiritual journey? *The word*

2. What must we do to be considered a disciple of Jesus? *Follow his one teaching*

3. What kind of knowledge will set us free? *experiential knowledge*

Chapter 1

1. What must happen for you to start your journey with Jesus, and go to heaven? *We must be born again*

2. What are the two essential components of mankind? *physical + spiritual*

3. How does knowing this help us diagnose our problems? *We see if it's under our control or not*

4. What third component do we get when the two essential components come together? *living being/soul*

5. We call the spirit and body essential components. What do we call the spirit, soul, and body? *tri-chotomy of man*

6. Of what does the image of God consists, and where do we find this image? *will, reason, emotions*

7. In what sequence should the capacities be?

8. What does it mean to be in the likeness of God?
   We use our capacities the way God does.

9. To what capacity of Eve did Satan appeal to get her to be disobedient? *reason*

10. What was lost in the fall of man, and what was retained?
    the source of life

11. What separates us from God?
    sin

12. From where does our reality come when we are separated from God? *the physical realm*

13. After the fall, what drove and controlled mankind?
    circumstances + emotions

14. Why did Jesus come to the earth?
    salvation

15. What are the three signs that someone is born again?
    testimony, love for truth/light, Jesus=king

16. Have you been born again? If you have, and if you are meeting with other people to do this study, why don't you share your testimony with the others?

Chapter Two

The Divine Rule

Although we have been born again, we have a way to go to develop Christlikeness in our lives. We are told in the scripture that we are to have the mind of Christ. When the Bible refers to the mind, it is safe to think of the soul, or the spiritual heart of man. We should see what the soul of an individual who has not been born again looks like. This person is biblically referred to as

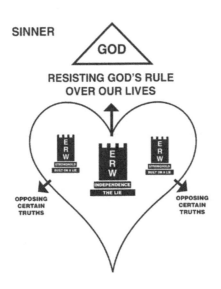

a sinner. The sinner will resist God's rule over his life. Not only does the sinner resist God's rule, he also doesn't desire it. The soul is filled with what we call strongholds which oppose certain biblical truths.

What is a stronghold? It is an attitude. According to Paul in 2 Corinthians 10:4-5, a stronghold is a pattern of thinking, generally satanically induced, that sets itself up against the knowledge of God. "The weapons we fight with are not the weapons of the world. On the contrary, they have divine power to demolish strongholds. We demolish arguments and every pretension that sets itself up against the knowledge of God." These patterns of thinking are formed by Satan at a certain point in time by sending lies to the capacity of reasoning usually to generate some type of emotion. The only thing that can tear down a stronghold is the divine weapon of truth.

An example of a stronghold that might exist in a sinner's life is the thought that he is not a sinner. But this is a pattern of thinking that sets itself up against the knowledge of God, and it might make us feel saved. God's truth says "for all have sinned and fall short of the glory of God" (Romans 3:23). Another possible stronghold might be the thought that there are multiple ways to heaven. But this is a satanically induced pattern of thinking that sets itself up against the knowledge of God. God's truth, while it is quoting what Jesus said, says, "I am the way and the truth and the life. No one comes to the Father except through me" (John 14:6).

We must understand that where there is a stronghold, the capacities of the soul (Will, represented by a W; Reason,

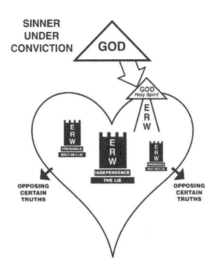

represented by an R; Emotions, represented by an E) do not function correctly—they are oriented upside down (E, R, W)—and the sinners will make their decision regarding salvation based on their emotions and false reasoning.

Many other patterns of thinking oppose God's word regarding the requirements to get into heaven. Regardless of what the lies are, the Holy Spirit will bombard these strongholds with God's truth. This is conviction in which the Holy Spirit attempts to convince us. Finally, the individual becomes convinced that God's word is true. The individual confesses, or agrees, and exchanges their deceptive pattern of thinking, which is a core part of the stronghold, for God's truth.

This change of mind is repentance. Therefore, **the individual confesses and repents, and the stronghold is torn down.**

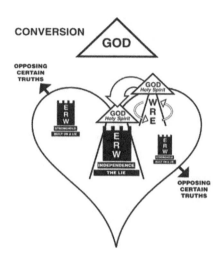

After the stronghold is torn down, the likeness of God is partially restored, and the capacities are partially oriented correctly, which means that a castle of grace (Will, Reason, Emotion) is constructed, and the Holy Spirit establishes a residence in the person's life. The individual is born again! This event might be called conversion, salvation, regeneration, or initial sanctification.

✳ Although the individual has been born again, and the Holy Spirit resides inside him, a number of strongholds still exist. These strongholds prevent complete freedom of the will, reason, and emotion: will create dissension in their relationships; or they may even prevent the development of godly relationships.

Now, although the Holy Spirit has established a new position on the inside to do his conviction, he will lead the person into all truth so that God's likeness can be restored in the person's life. But when he, the Spirit of truth, comes, he will guide you into all the truth (John 16:13a).

Now that we are born again we should start thinking differently, and changing our attitudes.

> So I tell you this, and insist on it in the Lord, that you must no longer live as the Gentiles do, in the futility of their thinking. They are darkened in their understanding and separated from the life of God because of the ignorance that is in them due to the hardening of their hearts. Having lost all sensitivity, they have given themselves over to sensuality so as to indulge in every kind of impurity, with a continual lust for more. You, however, did not come to know Christ that way. Surely you heard of him and were taught in him in accordance with the truth that is in Jesus. You were taught, with regard to your former way of life, to put off your old self, which is being corrupted by its deceitful desires; to be made new in the attitude of your minds; and to put on the new self, created to be like God in true righteousness and holiness. (Ephesians 4:17-24)

The Bible tells us that the way we used to think before we were born again is futile or worthless, and our actions are manifestations of our thinking. You have probably seen the bracelets that say "WWJD." These initials stand for "What Would Jesus Do?" A better question is "What Would Jesus Think?" We are told that in our former way of life we were emotionally driven. We are also told that we are to replace our old self with a new self, "created to be like God in true righteousness and holiness." This replacement is accomplished by making new the attitudes of our minds. We are to go from our old self to our new self

by— in what is a better translation of the original language—
the continual renewal of the spirit of the mind.

It is worth noting a couple of things. Paul says that the
new self was **"created to be like God"** and he also refers to
a **"true righteousness and holiness."** This latter part of the
verse is opposed to a false righteousness and holiness, that
which exists when we try to change ourselves from the outside without having our minds renewed. The phrase **"to be
made new,"** or renewal, is in the present tense. This means
that the renewal is an ongoing process that should continue.
It is a journey!

There are three different ways that a stronghold can become
established in a person's life. The destruction of these strongholds is an instantaneous event in which we exercise our wills
rather than a process. We will review all three, but we will deal
with only one in this chapter.

The first way is a bent that is a strong inclination or bias. I
might think a certain way because my mom and dad think that
way. They might think the way they do because their mom and
dad thought that way, and the same bent might be passed down
through the generations. For example, when I got married, I
thought that the time to celebrate Christmas was on Christmas
Eve because that was the day my family celebrated. My wife,
however, was raised celebrating Christmas on Christmas Day
after a big breakfast. Well, we didn't discuss this until about a
week before Christmas of our first year of marriage. Now, Satan
might not have induced these biases, nor may they be in dis-
agreement with God, but Satan sure used the difference to cre-

ate disunity in the Wards' house for a while. This is what Satan does when there are different biases in the church about various topics such as the style of worship. This is why everyone needs the mind of Christ, so there will be unity.

SINFUL NATURE

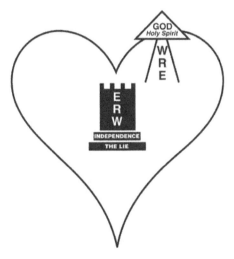

✴ There is one bent that is generational, and all of us have inherited it. In fact, theologically it is called inherited depravity, but the Bible calls it the sinful nature. It is an attitude or stronghold in the center of the heart. It is built on the pattern of thought that an individual can meet God's will for himself; or in other words, he can be like God when it comes to knowing good and evil. This attitude is the source of many other strongholds, because its independence is an open door for Satan's deception into one's life. This stronghold has passed down through all of the generations, and it started when Adam and Eve believed Satan's lie in the Garden of Eden. It is the original sin when the likeness of God was lost. When it speaks, it might sound like this: "I will do what I want, when I want, where I want, and how I want, if I do it at all." This is a very independent and selfish attitude, and Paul addresses it in Romans 7:14-8:2.

> We know that the law is spiritual; but I am unspiritual, sold as a slave to sin. I do not understand what I do. For what I want to do I do not do, but what I hate I do. And if I do what I do not want to do, I agree that the law is good. As it is, it is no longer I myself who do it, but it is sin living in me. I know that nothing good lives in me, that is, in my sinful nature. For I have the desire to do what is good, but I cannot carry it out. For what I do is not the good I want to do; no, the evil I do not want to do--this I keep on doing. Now if I do what I do not want to do, it is no longer I who do it, but it is sin living in me that does it.

> So I find this law at work: When I want to do good, evil is right there with me. For in my inner being I delight in God's law; but I see another law at work in the members of my body, waging war against the law of my mind and making me a prisoner of the law of sin at work within my members. What a wretched man I am! Who will rescue me from this body of death? Thanks be to God—through Jesus Christ our Lord!

> So then, I myself in my mind am a slave to God's law, but in the sinful nature a slave to the law of sin

> Therefore, there is now no condemnation for those who are in Christ Jesus, because through Christ Jesus the law of the Spirit of life set me free from the law of sin and death.

Before we start studying this passage, we should review the book of Romans up to this point. We are told that it doesn't matter whether you are a Jew or a Gentile, you have committed sin, and the only solution is the same for both; it is faith in Jesus. Then we are told that it doesn't matter whether you are a Jew or a Gentile, you have a diseased heart caused by the original sin, and the only solution is the same for both Jew and Gentile; it is faith in Jesus.

Then in Chapter 7, Paul starts talking about the Law of God that was given to the Jews. Although the Law cannot solve the problem associated with sin, it still serves a purpose. It is the Law that makes us aware that there is a sin problem. Paul says that this doesn't make the Law bad; the Law is good. Then in the Romans passage above, Paul refers to three different laws that exist. Now, he is not referring to God's Law to the Jews, but he has changed his definition, although the same word is used. Paul talks about "the law of the mind", "the law of sin", and "the law of the Spirit of life." When he refers to these three laws, he is referring to a law as a principle. This type of law states that given a certain set of conditions, a certain result will always be produced, without exception. You are probably familiar with at least one law of this type. One example is the law of gravity, which states that things will always fall to the ground unless there is an equal or greater opposite force applied to the object. We are told in the Scripture that the individual does not do what they want to do, but instead they do what they do not want. What the individual desires to do is the good and to be submissive to Jesus resulting from "the law of the mind" that became operational within the individual by the indwelling Holy Spirit. The Scripture tells us that the sin we commit is not actually being chosen by us, but instead, the sinful nature inside us, being pressured by "the law of sin" actually causes us to do things that we prefer not. This creates a real battle, or tug of war, within us. This passage can be very confusing causing many people to skip over it when they do their devotions or Bible study, but it holds the key to the freedom that we long for on our journey. We will spend some time to unpack it. If we take another look at a converted heart, then we can see all three laws in action.

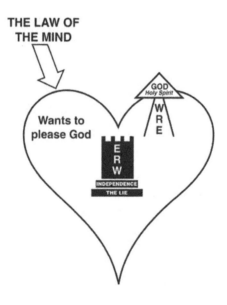

First is "the law of the mind." Every person who is born again will have the law of the mind. This comes from the Holy Spirit living in the heart when the new birth occurs. The scripture tells us that the individual delights in God's law.

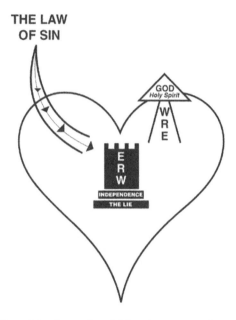

Secondly is "the law of sin." This law puts a force on the sinful nature of man, and it will always cause the individual to do some things that they do not desire. This law will make the individual a prisoner to it, and their sinful nature a slave to it. The sinful nature, while influenced by the law of sin, will be in conflict with the law of the mind.

These two laws, when operational, create a real battle within the individual. Now, we cannot do away with either one of these laws any more than we can do away with the law of gravity, but we can alter the item with which the law interacts.

**INNER
CONFLICT**

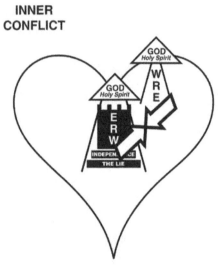

Third is "the law of the Spirit of life." This is available to everyone who is born again. It comes from the indwelling Holy Spirit. It can rescue us from the war and set us free from the powerful stronghold at the center of the heart, which is very independent and tries to control things by itself. We need to allow the Holy Spirit to be in charge of our lives.

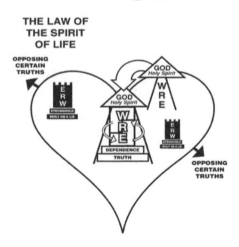

Imagine holding up and extended straight out from your body a book with one hand. You desire to keep the book from falling on the floor. It might start out easy, but as the downward pressure of the law of gravity works longer on the book, it becomes more difficult to keep from dropping the book. Even though you might drop the book because of the downward force, you just rest a while, pick the book up again, and continue with your original desire of keeping the book from falling to the floor. Now, you have a choice to make for your future attempts. Because you cannot eliminate the law of gravity, you can either try harder and focus more on your task, or you can get a helper to hold the book up for you. This is similar to our spiritual journey. After we are born again, we desire to do what is good because of the law of the mind, and we might start out on our journey meeting God's requirement of loving our neighbor as ourselves. "The entire law is summed up in a single command: 'Love your neighbor as yourself'" (Galatians 5:14). But, the longer we go, the harder it gets, because of the law of sin, which puts pressure on the sinful nature. Now, Satan will whisper in our ear that we should try harder and become more self-focused, or even start all over from the beginning. But, what we need is something done with the independent nature of the stronghold in the center of the heart. The key is to confess that we can't consistently meet the requirement, and we need the law of the Spirit of life to infiltrate our hearts. We need the Holy Spirit to do for us what we can't do for ourselves. We need to say yes to whatever the Lord might ask of us while we are on our journey before we know what he will ask of us. This is actually yielding completely to the Holy Spirit for his leading. The

Spirit of the Lord will immediately move to the center of the heart and tear down the independent stronghold (E, R, W) and convert it into a castle of grace (W, R ,E). The capacities of will, reason, and emotion are greatly freed, and the mind of Christ is grown.

> So I say, live by the Spirit, and you will not gratify the desires of the sinful nature. For the sinful nature desires what is contrary to the Spirit, and the Spirit what is contrary to the sinful natue. They are in conflict with each other, so that you dc not do what you want. But if you are led by the Spirit, you are not under law. (Galatians 5:16-18)

We need to continually yield ourselves to the Holy Spirit. "Then he said to them all: 'If anyone would come after me, he must deny himself and take up his cross daily and follow me'" (Luke 9:23).

If you have never prayed to yield your complete life—your dreams, your career, your time, your money, your marriage, your ministry, and everything about your self—or if you need to re-submit your life, then I suggest that you pray aloud this prayer.

PRAYER to YIELD to the SPIRIT

Dear Heavenly Father,

I want to thank you for the new spiritual birth that you have given me. I also want to thank you for giving me the Holy Spirit at the time of my new birth. I agree that I cannot meet your requirement for my life unless you do it for me. I want to yield my entire life to the Holy Spirit, and be a slave to him. I ask that the Holy Spirit lead me in pursuing the mind of Christ.

In Jesus' Name I Pray,

AMEN

CHAPTER 2
STUDY QUESTIONS

1. What does a sinner's heart resist?

2. What is a stronghold, as defined in this chapter?

3. What does a stronghold oppose?

4. Who forms these strongholds in our life?

5. What is the only thing that will tear down a stronghold?

6. Give a possible example of a stronghold in a sinner's life that would prevent him from becoming born again.

7. In what order are the capacities in a stronghold?

8. What does conviction mean?

9. What does confess mean?

10. What does repent mean?

11. When the stronghold is torn down, what happens?

12. How will strongholds impact our relationships?

13. Who leads us into all truth?

14. How was our thinking prior to becoming born again?

15. How do you go from the old self to the new self, and how long does it take?

16. How many different ways can a stronghold be created, and what type of stronghold is reviewed in this chapter?

17. What stronghold has been inherited by all people, and what does the Bible call it?

18. What are the three laws or principles reviewed by Paul in Romans 7?

19. When does the law of the mind take effect?

20. What law works on the sinful nature?

21. What two laws are in conflict?

22. How can we overcome the conflict?

23. What does the indwelling Holy Spirit make available to everyone who is born again?

24. What must we say to the Holy Spirit before he asks?

25. If you prayed a prayer to yield your life to the Holy Spirit, and if you are meeting with others to study this material, then why don't you share your experience with the others?

Chapter Three

The Forgiveness Grace

You were taught, with regard to your former way of life, to put off your old self, which is being corrupted by its deceitful desires; to be made new in the attitude of your minds; and to put on the new self, created to be like God in true righteousness and holiness.

Therefore each of you must put off falsehood and speak truthfully to his neighbor, for we are all members of one body. "In your anger do not sin": Do not let the sun go down while you are still angry, and do not give the devil a foothold. He who has been stealing must steal no longer, but must work, doing something useful with his own hands, that he may have something to share with those in need.

Do not let any unwholesome talk come out of your mouths, but only what is helpful for building others up according to their needs, that it may benefit those who listen. And do not grieve the Holy Spirit of God, with whom you were sealed for the day of redemption. (Ephesians 4:22-30)

**DEVELOPMENT
OF CHRIST-
LIKENESS**

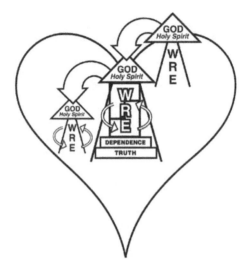

The scripture tells us that we need to be transformed by putting off the old self and by putting on the new self, by renewing our mind. The word used in the original language tells us that the renewal is an ongoing process. This process develops in us the mind of Christ. In fact, if there is any individual to whom we can't respond like Christ would, then we have a problem. That is what Christlikeness is all about.

This ongoing renewal or transformation is needed because of strongholds that have been established in our lives. These strongholds are patterns of thinking, generally satanically induced, that have set themselves up against the knowledge of God. They are located in the soul and they affect our capacities (Will, Reason, Emotion), which is the image of God. These strongholds prevent us from having Christlikeness in that particular affected area of our life, and we will be emotionally driven or circumstantially controlled when it comes to this particular issue in our life.

There are three different categories of strongholds. The first category, which we dealt with in the last chapter, is a bent or a strong inclination. We think a certain way about most things because we were taught that way. There is one pattern of thinking that we have inherited and were not taught. This pattern of thinking, or stronghold, is based on the lie that Adam and Eve believed which was, "you will be like God, knowing good and evil" (Genesis 3:5b). This lie has been inherited by all mankind and it will make us very independent and self-focused— it is known as the sinful nature. It is a big stronghold in the center of the spiritual heart, and it is influenced by the law of sin so that we do not do the good we want to do as born again individuals.

The second category of strongholds is due to spiritual wounds. These wounds or hurts come at us in a lot of different ways. Some individuals have been rejected, sexually abused, mentally abused, physically abused, told lies to and about, etc. The possibilities are too numerous to list them all. We need to be mindful that most hurts are done by those who are closest to us rather than by strangers. "If an enemy were insulting me, I could endure it; if a foe were raising himself against me, I could hide from him. But it is you, a man like myself, my companion, my close friend" (Psalm 55:12-13).

We should also remember that it does not have to be a big hurt, but it matters most how close to the heart the hurt is.

The way we must deal with these strongholds is by forgiveness. This is an area of our spiritual development that Satan wants us to resist and remain confused. For that reason, I think we should pause to ask God to make this material clear and protect us from all interference.

Sample Prayer

> Dear Heavenly Father,
>
> I ask that the blood of Jesus cover me so that all demonic interferences will be avoided. I ask that the Holy Spirit will bring clarity and simplicity to this material. I ask that any strongholds that have been able to form in my life because of spiritual hurts be demolished by your truth. I want to be set free.
>
> In Jesus' Name I Pray,
> AMEN

Many people believe they have a right to remain hurt, and they want to simply blame others for their unforgiveness, but this is not what the Scripture tells us. In fact, a number of Scriptures tell us just the opposite. Satan would like for us to think something different from what God's word has to say. After all, that is what a stronghold is. It is a satanically induced pattern of thinking that sets itself up against the knowledge of God. Keep in mind how Satan might appeal to our capacity of reasoning, and that he will try to deceive us in very subtle ways rather than with a flashing neon sign.

Forgiveness of others is so important that it is mentioned in Scripture a number of times.

> Get rid of all bitterness, rage and anger, brawling and slander, along with every form of malice. Be kind and compassionate to one another, **forgiving each other, just as in Christ God forgave you.** Be imitators of God, therefore, as dearly loved children and live a life of love, just as Christ loved us and gave himself up for us as a fragrant offering and sacrifice to God. (Ephesians 4:31-5:2)

> Bear with each other and **forgive whatever grievances you may have against one another, Forgive as the Lord forgave you.** (Colossians 3:13)

> **For if you forgive men when they sin against you, your heavenly Father will also forgive you.** But if you do not forgive men their sins, your Father will not forgive your sins. (Matthew 6:14, 15)

This passage from Matthew may be problematic for some individuals. If I interpret it correctly, Jesus is telling us that God will not forgive us if we refuse to forgive others that have offended us. Wow. We must also remember that an unforgiven person is an unredeemed person. Unfortunately, it is not unusual for people to reduce the meaning, as they might with other truths, to fit their personal preferences.

Based on these passages of Scripture, we can formulate a definition for forgiveness, and from that we can derive a definition for bitterness.

Forgiveness: to imitate God, through his grace, in matters of personal injury; to bestow a favor unconditionally.

Bitterness: to reject God's grace and example in my response to those who offend me.

As with some Scripture, it is not unusual for a person's pride and rebellion to slowly whittle away and reduce these definitions to the point of personal comfort.

I am going to share with you four simple biblical principles regarding your forgiveness of others that will help you on your pursuit of the mind of Christ. Remember this: you can finish this chapter and have more intellectual knowledge than before you started. But you can apply these principles to your life and experience the truth, and then the truth will set you free.

Principle #1. Forgiveness is a must for wholeness of life and relationship in a fallen world.

We should remember that our goal on our journey is to be made as whole as possible and to be able to have all the relationships that God wants us to have.

When I did pre-marital counseling, I would do my best to get the couple to become more acquainted with each other, but they had stars in their eyes and only saw this perfect person that they were about to marry. While the marriage was still tender, both of them would call me and would want to set an individual appointment with me. She would come to my office and ask me where the gentleman she married went. She would say, "He has changed." I would hear something similar from him when he shared about her. I would simply say, "Congratulations! You are getting to know the person you married." The best church marquee I can remember said, "A successful marriage is the union of two forgivers." We might find this to be true with all of our relationships as they develop.

You must understand that no relationship begins perfectly. In a fallen world, the only whole relationships are those that have been healed. In fact, this imperfect world will pressure the imperfect relationships composed of imperfect people, causing very imperfect understandings, attitudes, desires, and responses. You might be saying right now that I don't understand what has happened to you. You may be right, but I do understand what the Scriptures say.

> "Therefore everyone who hears these words of mine and puts them into practice is like a wise man who built his house on the rock. The rain came down, the streams rose, and the winds blew and beat against that house; yet it did not fall, because it had its foundation on the rock. But everyone who hears these words of mine and does not put them into practice is like a foolish man who built his house on sand. The rain came down, the streams rose, and the winds blew and beat against that house, and it fell with a great crash." (Matthew 7:24-27)

The storm or incident or circumstance is not the primary reason for the fall of the second house, rather it is a poor foundation. Don't blame the strength of the storm; rather, put your house on the solid foundation of God's word.

Principle #2. Forgiveness is an activity that always demands divine resources.

For us to be able to forgive, we need God's grace, which is a divine resource. In the following passage, the teachers of the law are correct when thinking that only God can forgive sins. But we are also told that God provides the divine resource necessary and mankind is to extend this resource to others.

> So many gathered that there was no room left, not even outside the door, and he preached the word to them. Some men came, bringing to him a paralytic, carried by four of them. Since they could not get him to Jesus because of the crowd, they made an opening in the roof above Jesus and, after digging through it, lowered the mat the paralyzed man was lying on. When Jesus saw their faith, he said to the paralytic, "Son, your sins are forgiven."
>
> Now some teachers of the law were sitting there, thinking to themselves, "Why does this fellow talk like that? He's blaspheming! Who can forgive sins but God alone?"

Immediately Jesus knew in his spirit that this was what they were thinking in their hearts, and he said to them, "Why are you thinking these things? Which is easier: to say to the paralytic, 'Your sins are forgiven,' or to say, 'Get up, take your mat and walk'? But that you may know that the Son of Man has authority on earth to forgive sins . . ." He said to the paralytic, "I tell you, get up, take your mat and go home." He got up, took his mat and walked out in full view of them all. This amazed everyone and they praised God, saying, "We have never seen anything like this!" (Mark 2:2-12)

The divine resource we need to forgive is grace. We can't break grace up and just use it to suit ourselves. We might like it better if grace was available to us from heaven in multiple spigots. If it was, we could open up the spigots for salvation, the Holy Spirit empowerment, and ministry, and we could leave the grace spigot closed when we need to forgive. Unfortunately, it doesn't work that way. You might say that grace comes out of one spigot, and when we close off the source of grace because we don't want to forgive, then we close off the source of grace we need for everything else, including salvation.

There are humanistic methods that we might try to use in place of extending grace. Keep in mind that when we are hurting, then our immediate goal is to feel better, and Satan will suggest one of the following so our emotions are satisfied.

Humanistic Methods of Forgiveness

1. Denial
2. Minimize
3. Rationalize
4. Justify
5. Pulverize

I think most of these are self-explanatory, except maybe pulverizing. Allow me to explain this one. Let's suppose that my wife tells me that when I get a certain look on my face I look like my father. Let's suppose that this causes a very imperfect reaction by me. My reaction might be to make a comment to my wife relating her looks or behavior to her mother. As a result she reacts to my hurtful comment with some negative and hurtful comment back at me. These back-and-forth hurtful comments might last for a while. This is pulverizing, and it might make us feel better, but it actually creates more wounds that will eventually need God's grace for healing.

I can remember one Saturday morning while living in Colorado Springs; I began to pray that God would show me any hurts that I might have from my childhood. After all, I was very blessed to have been in a loving, Christian home and didn't experience the wounds that some others have.

Speaking to my spiritual ears, the Lord said to me, "It was the corduroy pants." I asked, "What corduroy pants?" The Lord said, "The ones with which you started to school when you were six years old." He went on to say, "The ones that were three sizes too big, and you had to have them rolled up in three-inch cuffs, three times, and you wore them for three years, because you didn't grow for three years, and you felt goofy" I said, "Oh yes, I remember those corduroy pants." Then I began to justify and rationalize by saying, "Yeah, but Mom and Dad were just trying to be good stewards of the money, and besides that, they didn't know I wasn't going to grow for three years." The Lord responded, "You sure didn't think that way when you were six, seven, and eight years old." I said, "Yeah but, I love my mom and dad." The Lord said, "That's fine, it is okay to forgive those whom you love. In fact, you can consider that love and forgiveness is one and the same. They both originate with me." Well, after that brief dialogue, I got on my knees to pray and forgave my mom and dad for dressing me in those corduroy pants. Remember what I said earlier. It does not have to be a big hurt, but it matters most how close to the heart the hurt is.

> ". . .for love comes from God. . ." (1 John 4:7)

> "If anyone says, 'I love God,' yet hates his brother, he is a liar. For anyone who does not love his brother, whom he has seen, cannot love God, whom he has not seen. And he has given us this command: Whoever loves God must also love his brother." (1 John 4:20-21)

Principle #3. Forgiveness is always, first, a matter of choice (an act of the will).

Because forgiveness is a choice, I want to review what it is not.

Emotions: Forgiveness can't be based on our emotions because they are hurt. Our feelings might be telling us that we ought to take a baseball bat to the individual. Now, that might make us feel better, at least for a while. We shouldn't suppress our emotions though. We have a society full of people who suppress and deny their emotions with drugs and alcohol. The drugs don't have to be illegal either. All we have to do is to tell some doctors that we don't feel good, or we feel a little down, and they are quick to write us a prescription for a drug without checking for a physical cause.

After my stroke, the rehab doctor could not understand why I continually declined the antidepressants she continually prescribed for me. I finally told her that I believed that, if we could, we were meant to control our emotions instead of vice versa. If I couldn't, then I would take the medication to help me. Fortunately, I never had to start that prescription.

Our emotions should be an indicator, not a dictator, so they should not be masked or covered up. The emotions should indicate that something might be wrong; they should not dictate our response. They are like our indicator lights on our car's dash. Just because the "check engine" light comes on, it doesn't dictate we should take the car to the junk yard. And we certainly shouldn't smash out the light with our fist or cover it up with duct tape.

I delivered this message at one church in Washington State, and I was scheduled to go to breakfast the next morning with the pastor. The next morning, when I got in the pastor's car, the pastor said that he was a bit embarrassed because he had a piece of duct tape covering the "check engine" light.

Our emotions need to work because they are part of the image of God. The same capacity of emotion that makes us feel the pain from a hurt is the same capacity of emotion that I need to express God's love to others. That's why they say, "Hurting people hurt people." If we feel some negative emotion, this should not dictate our response to others. If our emotions indicate some negative feeling, then we should go to the Master Mechanic, let him open the hood to the heart, let him shine the light of truth on the problem, and allow him to fix the problem. After all of this, we can continue our journey without having to restart the journey from the beginning.

Trusting: Forgiveness doesn't mean trusting. In fact, it would be wise not to trust the person we forgive, unless we have reason to believe that God's grace has changed the individual and made them into a different person. When God commanded us to forgive, he never mentioned trusting. Forgiving and trusting are two different and distinct actions. The willingness to trust comes after forgiveness. Forgiveness is a prerequisite to trusting, but trusting is not a requirement for forgiveness. Why would we trust somebody who has hurt us? If the person hasn't been changed by God's grace, there is nothing to stop the person from doing something similar to us again. But God's grace can make the person a different individual, like he did us, and we should stand ready to restore trust to the new individual.

Excusing: Forgiveness is not as simple as us making excuses for the individual and justifying what they have done. This is what

I tried to do with my corduroy pants. It is not unusual for those involved in ministry to make excuses by rationalizing and justifying, because after all the offender is a baby Christian, and as mature ministering Christians, we should ignore those comments. When we do ministry we will get hurt; just look at Jesus!

Condoning: Forgiveness is not condoning what was done to us. There are many people who won't forgive because they believe that by doing so they are agreeing with what the person has done.

Conditional: Forgiveness is not conditional. I have heard many people say, "I will forgive them when they admit that what they have done is wrong," or, "I will forgive them when they say, 'I am sorry.'" Jesus did not forgive us conditionally. Yes, we must repent to receive the benefits of the forgiveness, but Jesus went ahead and granted forgiveness to everybody when he died on the cross. When we place a condition on granting our forgiveness, then we are appointing ourselves as the judge. Anytime we establish the guilt of someone else, then we have become the judge that is reserved for God.

Time Related: Forgiveness is not time related. Forgiveness is an instant choice. There are many who will say, "Time will take care of the forgiveness and the pain." This is one of Satan's big, but subtle, lies. A delay in time will only allow you to mask the pain with one of the humanistic methods. A delay will also allow a bitter root to spring up. Time will neither take the place of biblical forgiveness nor heal the hurt. Admit you're hurt, forgive, and go on.

God always directs his commands at man's will, and he will always empower a righteous choice. It is not human will-power, but a Holy Spirit empowered will that is the key to victory. If we want to evangelize where we live, we need to stop waiting for a nice warm and fuzzy feeling. We are to choose obedience, whether we feel like it or not.

Principle #4. Forgiveness is always a matter of <u>relationship</u> which involves another personality to which we must properly respond.

Holiness, or Christlikeness, means to be <u>other-focused</u> and to have the ability to respond to all people and God the Father as Christ would. Forgiveness cannot be an impersonal approach. Forgiveness should always involve a personality, instead of an institution or a group of people. We shouldn't hold a corporation, church, or family responsible for the actions of some. These are communities that consist of people, and these people have wills, and these people have chosen to say or do what they have said or done. It is to these individual personalities that God expects us to properly respond, s<u>o we need to forgive these people individually</u>.

> Make every effort to live in peace with all men and to be holy; without holiness no one will see the Lord. See to it that no one misses the grace of God and that no bitter root grows up to cause trouble and defile many. (Hebrews 12: 14-15)

This passage in other translations uses more aggressive words. It tells us to pursue or make every effort. The original language is very aggressive with the responsibility on our shoulders. Our responsibility is similar to what we are told in Romans 12. "If it is possible, as far as it depends on you, live at peace with everyone" (Romans 12:18).

Not only are we to make every effort to live in peace with all men, but we also are to make every effort to be holy. It then says that the absence of holiness will prevent us from going to heaven. There are many who believe that this holiness is a transcended holiness that is a vertical holiness between God and us, but it is not. It is a translated holiness that is a horizontal holiness between other people and us. We need to make every effort to have a right relationship with all people. According to Scripture, this is a must if we want to see the Lord. In other words, our relationships with other people affect our relationship with God.

The passage tells us that if a person does not use grace to maintain their relationships, then bitterness will develop quickly and become militant.

After all of this, you might say, "I think I have forgiven everyone who has offended me, but how do I know?" Well, there are passages in Matthew and Luke that can help us. In the following table, the left-hand column identifies our actions if we love or have forgiven our offender. The right-hand column identifies our actions if we have just learned to tolerate and have not actually forgiven our offender.

Love Your Offender	Tolerate Your Offender
Pray for them Matthew 5:44; Luke 5:28	Pray against them
Speak cordially to them Matthew 5:47	Ignore and avoid them
Keep no record of the debt Luke 6:30	Waiting to be repaid
Want them in heaven Matthew 5:44,45 Luke 6:37,38	Hope for their punishment
Speak well about them Luke 6:31,45	Rehearse offense to others
Do good deeds for them Luke 6:35	Refuse to offer help
See the beam in your own eye Luke 5:41-43	See the speck in others eye

We should pray for the one who offended us. First of all, it is not for us to determine the guilt of an individual, and just because someone's action may have offended us, it does not mean that their action is sinful in the eyes of God or that they are guilty in his eyes. If we have not forgiven the individual, then we might find ourselves actually praying against the individual. The first night I was scheduled at one church, an individual came to me and said, "Do you know how long it took us to pray the last pastor out of here?" I thought to myself, "God help them."

We should speak cordially to them, whenever we see them. If we have not forgiven the individual, then we might find ourselves actually ignoring or avoiding them. I remember one time that I went to the grocery store for my wife. I had my list, and

I was on a mission. All of a sudden, while looking down the aisles from the end aisle, I saw an individual who harasses me every time he sees me. Because I did not want to go through the harassment again, I went down a different aisle so that I could avoid him. The individual may have changed since the last time that I saw him, but I was looking at him through the eyes of a crushed spirit

We should keep no record of the debt. If we have not forgiven the individual, then we might find ourselves actually waiting for repayment. But all the repayment in the world will only give temporary relief. We are to the leave the repayment up to the Lord. "…for it is written: 'It is mine to avenge; I will repay,' says the Lord." (Romans 12:19)

We should want to actually see the individual in heaven someday. If we have not forgiven the individual, then we might find ourselves actually hoping for the individual's punishment. We are told that we are to bless those who curse us. I know of no better way to bless an individual than to pray that they will go to heaven. We should want to see everybody in heaven, because God certainly does. If we are hoping for their punishment, then we must have established their guilt. Frankly, being the judge is God the Father's job and not ours. This is sort of similar to the previous one in that it is God's offense to avenge.

We should speak well about them. If we have not forgiven the individual, then we might find ourselves actually rehearsing the offense to others. We are told in the Bible that we are to edify or build up each other.

I once had an appointment with a lady who had a troubled marriage. I knew that my colleagues had counseled with her quite a bit. Because of this, I knew that she probably would have heard most of the biblical principles I would use. But I also knew that a different voice and counseling style could make a difference. I counseled her husband the day before and had really gotten in his face, thinking he was not being the godly husband or head of the house that he should be. When I met with her the next day, she handed me an envelope that contained many notes and letters that her husband had written to her over the past twenty years. She was offended by some of them. She would occasionally review the contents of this envelope, and she would rehearse the hurtful ones—at least the ones that she thought were hurtful—with others, similar to how she was rehearsing them with me. She did this rehearsal, while at the same time she tried to convince me that she had forgiven her husband for all these past offenses and that all of their current marital problems were his fault. This type of rehearsal made it clear to me that the husband might not be the cause of their current problems after all. It became crystal clear to me that there was some unforgiveness remaining in her life.

We should offer them help when they are in a time of need. If we have not forgiven the individual, then we might find ourselves refusing to offer help to them when they need it.

We should see the beam in own eye. If we have not forgiven the individual, then we might see the speck in their eye. It is very interesting how critical of all people we can become when we have unforgiveness in our heart. We can be especially critical of the one who has offended us. We will see every little imperfection in the lives of others, while it is obvious, at least to others, that a very big flaw exists in our own life.

It is good to regularly review the above table of information during your quiet time with the Lord in order to determine if there is any unforgiveness in your heart. I want to encourage you to allow the Holy Spirit to lead you toward a person's name or incident, instead of making a witch-hunt list of them.

You might say, "How many times must I forgive the individual? The individual does the same thing every time they see me." Well, there is a Scripture passage that addresses this.

"Then Peter came to Jesus and asked, 'Lord, how many times shall I forgive my brother when he sins against me? Up to seven times?' Jesus answered, 'I tell you, not seven times, but seventy-seven times.'" (Matthew 18:21, 22)

The Jewish system, which is based on human effort, requires an individual to forgive seven times. But with grace, the number of times to forgive is unlimited. When we use grace for anything, then the amount that is made available to us is limitless.

I had a fellow ask me what happens when someone offends you after you have been forgiven. Under this scenario, are you then required to forgive? I knew he was thinking of Matthew 6:15 and that there was surely a way to beat the system. I answered him with an emphatic no and suggested that he read Matthew 18:23-35.

Therefore, the kingdom of heaven is like a king who wanted to settle accounts with his servants. As he began the settlement, a man who owed him ten thousand talents was brought to him. Since he was not able to pay, the master ordered that he and his wife and his children and all that he had be sold to repay the debt.

The servant fell on his knees before him. "Be patient with me," he begged, "and I will pay back everything." The servant's master took pity on him, canceled the debt and let him go.

But when that servant went out, he found one of his fellow servants who owed him a hundred denarii. He grabbed him and began to choke him. "Pay back what you owe me!" he demanded.

His fellow servant fell to his knees and begged him, "Be patient with me, and I will pay you back."

But he refused. Instead, he went off and had the man thrown into prison until he could pay the debt. When the other servants saw what had happened, they were greatly distressed and went and told their master everything that had happened.

Then the master called the servant in. "You wicked servant," he said, "I canceled all that debt of yours because you begged me to. Shouldn't you have had mercy on your fellow servant just as I had on you?" In anger his master turned him over to the jailers to be tortured, until he should pay back all he owed.

> This is how my heavenly Father will treat each of you
> unless you forgive your brother from your heart (Matthew
> 18:23-35).

If I have interpreted this passage of scripture correctly, then I would say that my forgiveness will be taken away if I refuse to extend forgiveness to those who have offended me. I also understand that I will be tormented if I don't forgive the people who have offended me.

This story really came alive to me one day while I served as an associate pastor in Colorado Springs.

A man, who I will call Henry, used to attend our church and was in one of our local hospitals with cancer. Not knowing if Henry currently had a local pastor, someone asked me to visit with him at Penrose Hospital. I went there and met Henry for the first time. After an introduction and a few cordial words, I didn't waste any time in asking Henry some questions in hopes that I could discern whether or not Henry was a Christian. My assessment was that Henry was a Christ follower. We visited on several different occasions until Pastor Dave came on our staff as the senior adults' pastor, then he started visiting Henry. In time, I actually lost track of Henry's prognosis, except I did know that he had been placed in the hospice care center due to his digression.

One Tuesday morning, once our weekly staff meeting was finished, Pastor Dave came running toward me waving a pink message slip. Pastor Dave said that he had a scheduled meeting that he must attend, and he asked me if I would handle the message he had in his hand. I said yes, then I read the message.

The message was from the chaplain of the hospice center. It read "Come quickly, Henry is in great spiritual distress." I couldn't imagine what possibly could be wrong with Henry, so I immediately got in my car and drove to the hospice center.

When I got there, I took the elevator to the third floor. When I stepped off of the elevator, I went right across the hall into Henry's room. There was a lady standing on the other side of the bed, and one of our saints from our church was standing on the door side. I introduced myself to the lady, and she did the same. I learned that she was Henry's ex-wife from two different marriages and divorces. In fact, she was Henry's caretaker in his last days. After a few cordial words with her, I leaned over the bed rail, and I said to Henry "Man, what is the problem?" Henry used a mechanical voice box and a hand held microphone to talk. For this reason, sometimes it could be difficult to understand what Henry was saying. He tried to answer me, but no one in the room could understand him. After Henry repeated himself about three times, his ex-wife finally understood what he was saying. Apparently, he was saying a man's name. His ex-wife said, "That is the name of your ex-truck-driving partner, and he has been dead for ten years; what does he have to do with anything today?" Henry held his microphone close to his throat and said clearly, so that we could all understand, "He had an affair with my wife." His ex-wife immediately replied, "Now, Henry, that incident was a long time ago, and besides, that was never proven." I knew that what his ex-wife had to say may make Henry feel better, but I wasn't interested in Henry *feeling* better, I wanted Henry to *be* better. I leaned over the bed rail again and said, "Henry, I believe that what you are experiencing right now

is torment because you are harboring bitterness or unforgiveness in your heart due to hurt caused by your ex-wife and your
former partner." I asked, "Are you willing to forgive your ex-
wife and this man?" At the age of seventy-two, Henry prayed a
prayer that I led him in, like thousands of others, and his chains
of bondage were broken. Henry was set free from the torment
that day.

You may have unforgiveness that is tormenting you. You
may have thought of a person, or an incident, where there is
unforgiveness, about half-way through this chapter. I encourage you to pray the following prayer out loud, word for word,
and get set free.

PRAYER to FORGIVE

Dear Heavenly Father,

*I choose to forgive (**name of person**) for (**name of hurt**). Without excusing them or condoning their actions, I release them and my rights to this hurt to you and for your judgment and mercy. I absolutely refuse to hold anything against them. I cancel any vows that I made to "get even" or to "never forgive." I ask you to heal the wounds to my spirit from this hurt and restore my relationship to you. Forgive my hatred and resentment and replace it with a love for (**name the person**). I want to see them in heaven.*

In Jesus' Name I Pray,

AMEN

You should pray this prayer for every offense and/or person that the Holy Spirit brings to your mind. Remember, you may not always feel better, but you did this with your will (your choice) not your emotions (your feelings). Also remember to explain the offense and name the person the best that you can. Don't be surprised if there is some resistance when you pray.

CHAPTER 3
STUDY QUESTIONS

1. Why do we need to put off the old self and put on the new self by renewing our mind? What does this develop?

2. Who should we respond like to all people?

3. Who has a problem if we can't respond properly to all people?

4. To what is the second category of strongholds due?

5. What do many people believe about their unforgiveness?

6. What matters most regarding the size of a hurt?

7. From what people do most hurts come from?

8. How do we get rid of this category of stronghold?

9. In what ways does Satan deceives us?

10. What does Jesus tell us will happen if we don't forgive?

11. What is forgiveness?

12. What is bitterness?

13. What will a person do to the meaning of some Scriptures and definitions?

14. What is a must for wholeness of life and relationship in a fallen world?.

15. How do all relationships begin in a fallen world?

16. What causes our lives to crumble in the storms of life?

17. What divine resource does forgiveness need?

18. From how many sources of grace are there to choose?

19. What grace do we sacrifice when we close off its source because we don't want to forgive?

20. What are some humanistic methods that are sometimes used in place of extending grace?

21. Of what is forgiveness always, first, a matter?

22. What is forgiveness *not*?

23. What should our emotions be?

24. What should our emotions not dictate?

25. Our emotions need to work because they are part of the image of God. What capacity that we feel the pain from a hurt is used to express God's love to others?

26. Are forgiving and trusting considered to be the same?

27. Should we stand ready to restore trust to an individual?

28. What do some people substitute for the actions that need forgiving?

29. What will a delay in time allow?

30. Who should we forgive for hurts?

31. What does holiness, or Christlikeness, mean?

32. What should we do to have a right relationship with all people.

33. What are some biblical indicators that we have not forgiven?

34. How many times must I forgive an individual?

35. What will happen to the forgiveness given to me if I refuse to forgive others?

Chapter Four

The Repentance Grace

Our goal should be to become mature ministering Christians. To become this, we need an on-going work of Christlikeness in our lives by the demolishing of strongholds. This demol-

MATURE
MINISTERING
CHRISTIAN

ishing is the on-going renewal of the mind that is referenced in Ephesians 4:23 with the words to be made new in the attitude of your minds. These strongholds are patterns of thinking, or attitudes, generally satanically induced, that set themselves up against the knowledge of God. The only thing that can demol-

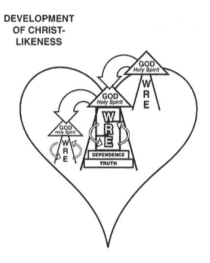

DEVELOPMENT OF CHRIST-LIKENESS

ish these strongholds is the divine weapon of truth. There are three different ways that a stronghold can be established in our lives. One way is by a bent. We can think a certain way because of the way we were taught or by being born with it. We dealt with this type of stronghold in Chapter 2. Another way that a stronghold can be established is by a spiritual or emotional hurt. We dealt with this type of stronghold in Chapter 3.

The third way that a stronghold can be established is by some sin committed by us, which we will review in this chapter of repentance. This is also a wound to the spirit, but I like to call it a self-inflicted one.

Paul takes much of his second letter to the Corinthians defending himself and his teaching against the "super apostles" that had come to Corinth. These super apostles were actually false teachers, who claimed to be apostles, and they tried to discredit Paul as an apostle, and his ministry including his teaching, and they were teaching some bad stuff. They poisoned the believers' minds with a watered-down gospel, and Paul accuses them of peddling the gospel for a profit. The Greek word used for "peddling" is the same one used to refer to those individuals who watered down their wine to make more money. There was definitely a distortion of God's word, and the ultimate result was that some believers accepted certain lifestyles and behaviors of the world. Because of the way some believers handled their guilt, strongholds or patterns of thinking would develop, and they would accept and live by some standards of the world. "When the sentence for a crime is not quickly carried out, the hearts of the people are filled with schemes to do wrong" (Ecclesiastes 8:11).

Paul halted his arguments about his credentials compared to those of the so-called super apostles. After all, speaking God's truth without watering it down was the most important qualification. Paul said that everything that he did was for the strengthening of the believers.

> Have you been thinking all along that we have been defending ourselves to you? We have been speaking in the sight of God as those in Christ; and everything we do, dear friends, is for your strengthening. For I am afraid that when I come I may not find you as I want you to be,

and you may not find me as you want me to be. I fear that there may be quarreling, jealousy, outbursts of anger, factions, slander, gossip, arrogance and disorder. I am afraid that when I come again my God will humble me before you, and I will be grieved over many who have sinned earlier and have not repented of the impurity, sexual sin and debauchery in which they have indulged (2 Corinthians 12:19-21).

What we actually find in this passage are the fruits or manifestations of a stronghold. There will always be at least one of the fleshly works produced by a stronghold. Paul tells the people of Corinth he is afraid that he might see in operation certain works of the flesh that we find as the manifestation of the sinful nature. These fleshly works can be found in several passages of the Bible, and what follows are two of those lists.

The acts of the sinful nature are obvious: sexual immorality, impurity and debauchery; idolatry and witchcraft; hatred, discord, jealousy, fits of rage, selfish ambition, dissensions, factions and envy; drunkenness, orgies, and the like...(Galatians 5:19-21a)

Get rid of all bitterness, rage and anger, brawling and slander, along with every form of malice. (Ephesians 4:31)

Paul lists certain behaviors that might exist, but he identifies three specific ones from their past for which they have not repented. We need to study a little closer this idea of repentance. So many of us might think that repentance is an activity only for salvation, but this grace—repentance—is what we need to demolish strongholds and to develop the mind of Christ. Therefore, repentance should be a normal ongoing part of the Christian's life.

There are five questions about repentance that I will answer.

What Is Repentance?

The literal definition is "a change of mind." It is the arrival of a different view about something. Except for one time, in the New Testament it always refers to sin. So, it is the arrival of a different view about a sin. Now, just any view is not good enough. We should not seek our pastor's, our church's, our parents', our friends', or definitely not the world's view. Although these views may be right, we should seek the Jesus-view about a sin. So, repentance is the arrival of the Jesus-view about a sin. Why should we listen to the pastor's sermon, or read the Bible, or be exposed to any of God's truth, if we are not ready to repent? In fact, as Christ-followers, every day we should long for repentance.

How can we teach anybody else, including our children, if we haven't arrived at the Jesus-view about sin? How can we be in one accord with others if we both are not united with Jesus in our views about sin?

Why Is Repentance Necessary?

Repentance is necessary because of the residual effects of sin. Notice what Paul said: *"I will be grieved over many who **have sinned earlier and have not repented. . ."** (2 Corinthians 12:21). The verb that is translated "have sinned earlier" is in the

Greek perfect tense. When a verb is in this tense, it speaks of an action that took place and was completed in the past, but we experience some result in the present. For instance one might say, "I have closed the door" which speaks of a past, completed action. But the implication is that, as a result, the door is still closed. Thus, the entire meaning is, "I have closed the door, *and it is closed at the present time.*" There are relatively few of these verbs in the New Testament, but when there is one, it usually has great theological truths associated with it. For another example, we can look at John 19:30, in which Jesus said *"It is finished."* This is a verb in the perfect tense. Jesus died on a cross in the past, and he will never do it again, but we benefit from this past action in the present. Praise the Lord!

So what Paul is actually saying is. I fear that there may be quarreling, jealousy, outbursts of anger, factions, slander, gossip, arrogance and disorder (consequences in the present). I am afraid that when I come again my God will humble me before you, and I will be grieved over many who have sinned earlier (completed a sin in the past and you are still having consequences in the present) and have not repented (arrived at the Jesus-view about what you have done in the past) of the impurity, sexual sin and debauchery in which they have indulged (past actions that are not being done in the present).

I want to emphasize that the individuals may have been forgiven and born again, but they still may not have arrived at the Jesus-view for what they have done in their pasts. This is like me driving railroad spikes into the nice walls of your home. You probably would tell me to get rid of them because they are not consistent with the look you wanted to project.

So I pull out the spikes, and I never again drive spikes into your walls again. You come home to see that the spikes are gone, and you are glad; but there are now ugly holes in your walls. You would probably tell me to get the walls patched and painted so the walls can be returned to their original state. This is similar to past sins in our lives. We can be forgiven for what we have done, and we can get out of the sin business, but there still may be some residual effects of the past and completed sins, if repentance has not been complete. We need the Master Carpenter to come along with his grace to patch some holes. This will help return us to our original state. This will help us develop the mind of Christ.

When we sin, God will, because of his determination of our guilt, through our conscience, place the emotion of shame on us in hopes that we will turn to the cross of Christ. We can rid ourselves of this emotion of shame by accepting the repentance granted to us. If we have previously repented for this particular activity, then Satan might just be accusing us and creating a false shame as a result of false guilt. When Satan does this, then we should quote to him 1 John 1:9: "If we confess our sins, he is faithful and just and will forgive us our sins and purify us from all unrighteousness." If we don't repent, we still want to rid the feeling of shame from ourselves. Satan will have us do something other than repent so that the feeling will go away. Our emotions can be affected by what we think. Therefore, Satan might suggest the following to get us to think a certain way so that our feeling of shame will go away.

Blame-shifting: This is done when we don't want to take responsibility for our choices. This approach of justifying and rationalizing is the oldest approach. Eve used this approach in the Garden of Eden, because she didn't want to take responsibility for her own choice. Unfortunately, this approach is very popular among all people. Oftentimes, people will compromise their moral values because of their careers or their finances, and they might blame their bosses for their decisions.

Legalism: This is what I like to call "the list." When our conscience tells us that we have sinned, Satan will tell us that we ought to check the list if we want to feel better. In checking the list, we find that we are not doing all the things on the list that we shouldn't do, such as smoking, drinking, going to the movies, etc. We find ourselves doing all of the good, positive things on the list, such as going to church, reading the Bible, praying, etc. The list will always include our views of what the Christian life should look like. When we grade our performance using the list as the standard, we will always score an A plus, and we will feel better.

Humanism: This takes God and his definition of sin completely out of the picture. If it is acceptable to society, then it is okay. One of the ways we do this is by calling it something else. We might even deny that we ever have committed the sin. This approach is very popular among Christians. I remember when a pastor's wife told me that the only thing she didn't like about her job was that sometimes she had to stretch the truth. That is one way of denying that she lied. We just redefine our actions.

Willful Ignorance: This is when we voluntarily or willfully stay ignorant as to what God considers to be a sin.

I have actually had Christians tell me that they really didn't want to know what God thought about a particular situation because they had already made up their mind to do that particular activity.

Minimize: This is when we rank the sins. We will always put at the top of the "worse" column the sins that we don't practice. Of course, we put at the top of the "not-so-bad" column the ones that we practice regularly. I've got news for you: all sins are the same with the Jesus-view. All of them will separate you from God.

Conscience Searing: This will happen if we ignore God's prompting to repent long enough. God uses our consciences to communicate our guilt to us. This communication will create in us the feeling of shame. If we ignore this feeling of shame long enough, it is possible to deactivate, or sear, our conscience.

Party Making: This is getting others to agree with us. If this approach is used within the church, then it can lead to a church split. Imagine that two people within the church are in a carnal debate with each other. They both should repent for their actions to feel better, but instead they both solicit supporters for their side of the issue. As long as one of the individuals has at least one more person on their side than the other individual, then that particular individual will feel more in the right and as a consequence, better. Of course, this feeling goes away when the other individual gets one more person on their side.

I remember when a counselee was about to make a decision that conflicted with God's word. She came back the next day and informed my wife and me that her father and a friend agreed with her decision, as if their agreement made the decision right. Of course, we will only approach for reinforcement people we know will be sympathetic to our view.

What Does Repentance Stress?

Repentance stresses the mind, or the entire being of mankind—the will, reason, and emotion. It does not stress the physical part of mankind only. In the Old Testament, repentance consisted of a physical turning and separation from the sin. Now, this is good, but it does not go far enough. An entire sect of people, known as the Essenes, relocated to the desert to isolate themselves from the sins of the world. This isolation alone will not work. In fact, God does not want us to be isolated; rather, he wants us to be insulated. Jesus prays this in his prayer to the Father in John 17:15-18: "My prayer is not that you take them out of the world but that you protect them from the evil one. They are not of the world, even as I am not of it. Sanctify them by the truth; your word is truth. As you sent me into the world, I have sent them into the world."

For repentance to be complete, we need to not only choose (our will) to separate ourselves from a sin, we need to feel (our emotions) like Jesus does about that sin, and we need to think (our reason) like Jesus does about that sin. This will help develop the mind of Christ.

If sin was a physical element only, then there would be a physical solution. For example, if sin was a physical thing, then we would have individuals in white coats at all church services and seminars. Anybody convicted of a sin would have one of the people in the white coats do an operation and cut out the sin.

Sin is spiritual, and it requires a spiritual solution. Jesus makes the difference very clear between the Old Testament view of sin and the New Testament view of sin. He reminded some that they might say that you shouldn't commit murder—that's physical; but in the New Testament, Jesus says that you shouldn't even be angry with your brother—that's spiritual. He also reminded some that they might say that you shouldn't commit adultery—that's physical; but in the New Testament, Jesus says that you shouldn't even look at a woman lustfully—that's spiritual. In other words, your name may be listed in the murder section or in the adultery section of the *Jesus Daily Journal*, if you have anger for your brother or look lustfully at a woman.

> You have heard that it was said to the people long ago, "Do not murder, and anyone who murders will be subject to judgment." But I tell you that anyone who is angry with his brother will be subject to judgment. . .
>
> You have heard that it was said, "Do not commit adultery." But I tell you that anyone who looks at a woman lustfully has already committed adultery with her in his heart (Matthew 5:21-22 ,27-28)

What Does Repentance Produce?

Scripture tells us that repentance, when complete, will produce fruit or deeds "Produce fruit in keeping with repentance" (Matthew 3:8). There will always be a behavioral change. Paul tells us in 2 Corinthians what some of the other fruit will look like.

"See what this godly sorrow has produced in you: what earnestness, what eagerness to clear yourselves, what indignation, what alarm, what longing, what concern, what readiness to see justice done. At every point you have proved yourselves to be innocent in this matter" (2 Corinthians 7:11).

I have put this verse into a table so that you can see the difference between godly sorrow, which will lead us to repentance, and its opposite, worldly sorrow or remorse, which will lead us to death.

Repentance 2 Corinthians 7:11	
Godly Sorrow	**Worldly Sorrow**
Earnestness towards repentance	Casual attitude towards repentance
Eager to clear oneself of the sin	Hiding the sin
Indignation for the sin	Sympathetic for the sin
Great alarm for the consequence	Spiritually dull to the effect
Long to be restored to man and God	Longing for relief from the guilt
Concern for the injured	Concern for self
Ready to see justice done	Resisting justice

We are told that if we have really repented, then we will take it seriously; otherwise, we will be insincere or casual about the need for repentance.

We are told that if we have really repented, we will be eager or very aggressive to get the sin openly revealed and to clear ourselves; otherwise, we will want to hide the truth about our actions. We should never hide the truth; instead, we should let God's light shine on our lives. This is considered to be transparency.

There was a pastor's wife who thought that her husband was sexually innocent when they got married, even though he wasn't. For years the pastor continually hid the truth from his wife knowing that she believed his lie. He was not eager to truly repent of his earlier sexual sin. As time passed, it might have been easier to live with the past, but the pastor had not reached the Jesus-view about his past sin. After being convicted of this truth, and believing that the Lord had prepared the way, he told his wife about his long time secret. The revealed truth did understandably create some tension in their relationship, which required grace by her to forgive. When he completed his repentance, he had a freedom and a power to minister like never before. Although this truth did hurt his wife, she was healed by God's grace by the forgiveness for the offense, and they developed a stronger relationship than they had before. Praise the Lord, there was nothing hidden between them any longer! The truth had set them both free.

We are told that if we have really repented, then we will be indignant to the sin; otherwise, we will be sympathetic to the sin.

If we are sympathetic to a sin, then it will be very difficult to discuss the indignity associated with it with other people. It is not likely that we will discuss this one with our children, grand-children, small group, etc. It is not likely that a pastor would include this particular sin in his sermons.

I remember in one service saying that even if two people were engaged and claimed to be Christians, if they were having premarital sex, then it had to be lust instead of love, because love came from God, and there was no way he would provide his resources on an ungodly activity. A lady came to me after the service and questioned my statements about love versus lust, not wanting to accept the truth I had shared. I repeated myself and shared what the Scripture had to say. She was not prepared to readily receive God's word, and she said that she would have to think about it. Now, there was some reason why she initially opposed God's truth on this matter. It could have been a satanically induced pattern of thinking, which is a stronghold that had developed years ago to deal with shame, if she had premarital sex while she claimed to be a Christian and was engaged. For whatever reason, she did not have the Jesus-view about the sin. She would also find it difficult, if not impossible, to tell her own daughter that premarital sex is a sin in any circumstance.

If we were really indignant about a sin, then we wouldn't find it entertaining to watch, listen, or read about.

If we have really repented, then we will be greatly alarmed about the consequences the unrepented sin creates; otherwise, we will be spiritually dull about the consequences. Unrepented sin will always have a negative effect on our development of the mind of Christ. Our spiritual growth and progress should be of great importance to us, and anything that hinders this progress should cause us great alarm.

If we have really repented, then we will long to be restored to God and the other people we have offended; otherwise, we will only long to be relieved from our guilt. This is so close to the next sign that I want to discuss them together. If we have really repented, then we will be concerned for the injured people; otherwise, we will only be concerned for ourselves. We will always want all of our relationships to be as whole as possible. If we have done anything that has directly offended anyone, then we should be more concerned about the fractured relationship than our own guilt. If we have completely repented, then we will be concerned about the injured people rather than being self-focused. I remember several years ago when a public official claimed to have repented for some of his actions. However, the individual demonstrated a self-focus with a concern for how the sin was going to impact him and his own career more than the impact on the offended lives.

We might think that our sin doesn't affect another person. But, if our sin prevents God from using us to minister to other individuals, then there are other people affected. And, we should remember that any time we have sinned against another individual then, we have sinned against God. There are some people who think that their relationship with God is the only thing that matters.

If we have really repented, then we will be ready for justice to be done; otherwise, we will resist justice. You would like to know what will be considered just, but that's just the issue.

You don't know what the process will be, but you should be willing to submit to the process regardless of what it is. It will probably require some type of restitution to the injured party or parties.

We ought to be able to use this table to determine if we have completely repented. I encourage you to reference this table frequently during your quiet time with the Lord. I would not make a self-generated list; instead, allow the Holy Spirit to bring to your mind whatever he wants you to address. Remember, if you are feeling shameful for something that you have completely repented, then you are probably experiencing false guilt. When this happens, quote and believe 1 John 1:9.

How Is Repentance Possible?

"Those who oppose him he must gently instruct, in the hope that **God will grant them repentance** leading them to a knowledge of the truth" (2 Timothy 2:25).

Repentance is only possible by God's grace. The scripture tells us that God grants repentance. This means that it is a gift of God. Remember, we can't break grace up and use it to suit ourselves. We might like it better if grace were available to us from heaven in multiple spigots that would allow us to use grace only when we want. You might say that grace comes out of one spigot, and when we close off the source of grace because we don't want to repent, then we close off the source of grace we need for everything else including salvation. God makes it possible for us to have a Jesus-view about a sin.

I encourage you to pause right now and allow the Holy Spirit to highlight a sin that God wants to grant to you a Jesus-view about that sin. I have included a sample prayer for your use.

PRAYER of REPENTANCE

Dear Heavenly Father,

*I confess that I have committed the sin of (**name the sin**). I accept the repentance you grant me, and I renounce my past involvement in this sin, and by your grace I absolutely refuse to be involved again. I take back all the ground I have given the devil by my spiritual rebellion, and I yield myself unreservedly to You, Lord Jesus. I am willing to walk through whatever process is necessary, including any needed restitution toward others, to produce the fruit in keeping with repentance.*

In Jesus' Name I Pray,

AMEN.

You should pray this prayer for every incident that the Holy Spirit brings to your mind. Remember, you may not always feel better, but you did this with your will (your choice) not your emotions (your feelings). Also remember to call the sin the same as Jesus does in his word.

CHAPTER 4
STUDY QUESTIONS

1. As Christians, what should be our goal?

2. What do we need to meet our goal?

3. What is the third way a stronghold can be established?

4. What will a stronghold produce?

5. We know that truth is needed to demolish strongholds. How is grace used to change these strongholds in to castles of grace?

6. Of what should repentance be a normal on-going part?

7. What view should we have about sin?

8. Why is repentance necessary?

9. What kind of effect can unrepeated sin have?

10. What do we call it if Satan accuses us after we have repented?

11. What Bible verse should we quote if Satan accuses us after we have repented?

12. Explain what Satan might do so that our feeling of shame will go away?

13. What does New Testament repentance stress?

14. Instead of us being be isolated, what does God want us to be?

15. What do we need to do for repentance to be complete?

16. What is sin and what kind of a solution does it need?

17. What does repentance produce?

18. What are some of the fruits given to us in 2 Corinthians?

19. Discuss what signs exist if repentance has not taken place.

20. Is there any time that a sin can be private and not affect anybody else?

21. What justice should we be ready to see done?

22. What is the only way that repentance is possible?

APPENDIX A

Anatomy of a Stronghold

Before we start discussing how a stronghold is constructed, we should review the definition of a stronghold. It is a pattern of thinking, generally satanically induced, that sets itself up against the knowledge of God. One of the works of the flesh will be manifested by the stronghold. The works of the flesh are a result of the stronghold in the center of the heart which acts like a feeder. This stronghold has been inherited by all mankind, and it is known as the sinful nature. We need to understand the anatomy of this stronghold because all other strongholds are

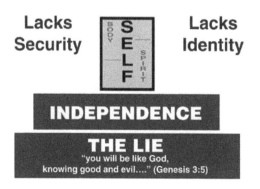

Identity and Security based in people, power, position, performance, fame, wealth, etc.

the result of the independence of this one. Strongholds don't actually consist of a will, reason, and emotion, but the strongholds do affect these capacities. Since the stronghold in the center of the heart acts as a feeder, we should study this one first. The individual has inherited the lie that *". . .you will be like God, knowing good and evil. . ."* (Genesis 3:5), and this foundational lie will cause the individual to be very independent. Since they have inherited the lie and are very independent, the individual will try to meet their identity and security needs by themselves.

False Sources of Identity and Security produce fears.

As a result of this independence, the individual will turn to the wrong things for these needs to be met. The independent individual will choose false sources of identity and security, such as power, position, people, performance, wealth, fame, etc. All such items are not true security and identity sources, and can be considered a lie. Because these things are false sources and can be lost, a fear of them being lost will be established. Because of the fear, a vow may be made so that the lie may be protected. The vow that we make may produce a mindset that will oppose certain truths. This mindset will also produce certain habits. The earlier in life that this independent center stronghold is destroyed, the better off we are, because the independent and self-focused nature will be an open door for Satan's deceptions to establish more strongholds as our life progresses. All other strongholds will be constructed similarly in that they will tend to be independent. At the root, or in the core, there

will be a sin, wound, or bent that is a strong inclination or bias. These are the three categories of a stronghold. Satan will offer us a lie to cover up and protect what is at the root. Imagine being at a busy intersection in a city during the afternoon rush

hour. With cars passing on both sides, you realize that you are naked. Someone comes by and notices your rather awkward position. The passer-by offers you a towel to cover up. You notice that the towel is quite dirty with grease and dried paint, but you don't turn it down to wait for a clean white towel. You take the dirty towel and cover up. This cover-up meets your need to eliminate the feelings that you have due to your public condition. This is similar to Satan offering us a dirty lie that comforts our feelings that may be caused by a wound, sin, or bent. If our need is to have our emotions comforted, and if we are emotionally driven, then we will not wait for the truth. If this happens, a stronghold construction begins, and we will become more emotionally driven.

With the dirty towel wrapped around me, and my emotional needs met, I might be fearful that you will take the towel from me, and I might make a vow that I will never be caught

in public again without being fully clothed. In fact, if my house catches on fire in the middle of the night, I might find it almost impossible to escape the burning house without becoming fully clothed first. It is the same with other areas of our lives, if we make a vow. For example, we might get emotionally hurt while we are doing some type of ministry. To protect ourselves in the future, we might make a vow that we will never do ministry again. The real problem arises when we realize it is God's will for us to do the very ministry in which we received the prior hurt. This same scenario can happen with marriage, if we make a vow to never remarry after an unforgiven hurt from a prior marriage. Do you know how many people are not doing God's will in their lives because of some past vow?

After we make a vow, we might develop a certain mindset. We will interpret and evaluate other people and institutions

through this way of thinking. The established mindset might make it difficult-to-impossible to have proper relationships with others.

After a mindset has been developed, we will probably oppose certain truths. The truths that we will oppose are the ones that challenge the lies we believed in the beginning, that we used to comfort our emotions. After all, this opposition to certain truths is a key indicator that a stronghold exists.

Because of this opposition, we might develop certain habits and feel some resistance while dealing with a stronghold. Even if a passer-by were to come along later with a clean, white towel, it is not likely that you will readily make the swap. To do so, you would have to momentarily uncover yourself, causing you to feel the original emotion all over again. This is the same way it works when we exchange a lie for the truth. It is not necessarily easy to pursue the mind of Christ.

APPENDIX B

A Castle of Grace

We want to tear down the strongholds and replace each of them with a castle of grace. When this is done, some of the lost likeness is restored. This process is the development of Christlikeness or the mind of Christ. The tearing down of the stronghold and the replacing it with a castle of grace is accomplished by exchanging the core lie with the opposing truth. The independent center stronghold that is based on the lie from Genesis is torn down and replaced with a castle of grace based on complete dependence on God and the truth of John 14:6: "I am the way." This exchange is done by praying the prayer of complete dependence on the Holy Spirit. The other exchanges are done by forgiving and repenting.

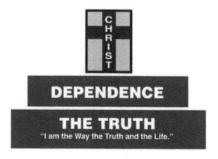

Every layer on top of the lie is an indicator that a stronghold exists. The replacement of the lie with God's truth is our ultimate goal. This might require us to deal with some of the layers on top of the lie first.

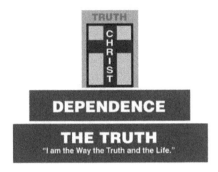

Once the lie is replaced with God's truth, then we can replace the fear with faith. We have no need for fear, because God's truth will not change, therefore it is faithful whereas the lie is not.

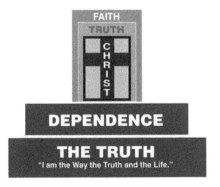

We, at some point in time, need to cancel or renounce the vow that we made to protect ourselves. We need to replace this vow by declaring a covenant with God that we will do his will.

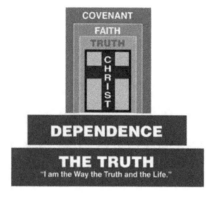

As the result of faith in God's truth and our covenant with God, our mind of Christ will be enlarged.

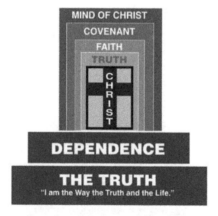

The larger our mind of Christ is, the more we will love the truth, and the more fruit we will manifest.

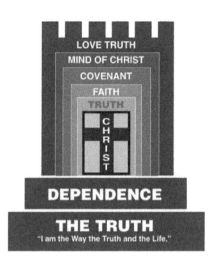

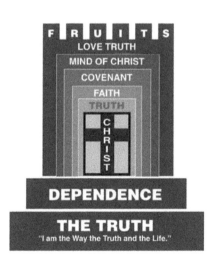

APPENDIX C

Leader's Guide

You may want to study this material in a group setting. The purpose of this section is to provide the group leader with suggestions about how the material could be segmented for the number of weeks allotted for the study. This section will also provide the leader with suggestions about how the time might be used.

Four-Week Sermon Series

I would make this a four-week sermon series with each chapter representing a sermon. I would not preach a sermon from appendices A and B. You might consider having the prayers typed on cards for distribution at the close of the service. The prayer cards for forgiveness and repentance should be distributed to all people for them to become isolated and allow the Lord to identify what should be dealt with. You probably will want to allow thirty minutes to an hour for the sermon. If you would like the illustrations and tables in Power Point format, please e-mail me at daleward@freedomquest.org and I will send them to you via e-mail.

Four-Week Small-Group Study

You probably should not attempt to do the study in a four-week session unless you have two hours per lesson, including the question and answer session. I would not attempt to study the appendices, although group members might want to peruse these sections on their own. The questions usually have one right answer that can be given. Remember to try to get everybody to participate. I encourage you to allow the individuals to give their testimonies regarding the chapter at the end of each session.

6 Week Small Group Study

This is similar to the four-week session. You might take the additional two weeks to discuss appendices A and B, and any other topics in the chapters about which individuals have questions.

8 Week Small Group Study

You might consider this format if you only have about 1-1½ hours for the study, and the questions and answers. I suggest doing about ½ of each chapter and ½ of the questions per session. You will want to split the chapter and their questions at a logical place. I would not attempt to discuss the appendices but would encourage the individuals to peruse these sections on their own.

10 Week Small Group Study

This is similar to the eight-week session. You might take the additional two weeks to discuss appendices A and B, and any other topics in the chapters about which individuals have questions.

Regardless of the study format chosen, try to get everybody to participate, and encourage individuals to give their testimonies regarding the chapter at the end of each session.

Ordering Books

Please go to www.freedomquest.org to order additional copies of this book.